The Urbana Free Library

To renew: call 217-367-4057
or go to "*urbanafreelibrary.org*"
and select "Renew/Request Items"

Can You See a Chimpanzee?

I'm the Cat in the Hat,
and we must not be late.
Today I will take you
to meet a primate.

The Cat in the Hat's Learning Library® introduces beginning readers to basic non-fiction. If your child can read these lines, then he or she can begin to understand the fascinating world in which we live.

Learn to read. Read to learn.

This book comes from the home of

THE CAT IN THE HAT

RANDOM HOUSE, INC.

For a list of books in **The Cat in the Hat's Learning Library**, *see the back endpaper.*

To the wonderful readers and writers in
Mystic and Groton, Connecticut.
Keep reading and writing!
—T.R.

The editors would like to thank
BARBARA KIEFER, Ph.D.,
Charlotte S. Huck Professor of Children's Literature,
The Ohio State University, and
CHRISTOPHER COE, Ph.D.,
Professor, University of Wisconsin–Madison,
for their assistance in the preparation of this book.

Visit us on the Web!
Seussville.com
randomhouse.com/kids

Educators and librarians, for a variety of teaching tools, visit us at
RHTeachersLibrarians.com

Library of Congress Cataloging-in-Publication Data
Rabe, Tish.
Can you see a chimpanzee? : all about primates / by Tish Rabe ;
illustrated by Aristides Ruiz and Joe Mathieu. — First edition.
   pages cm. — (Cat in the hat's learning library)
Includes bibliographical references.
Summary: "Join the Cat in the Hat as he explores the amazing world of chimpanzees." —
Provided by publisher.
ISBN 978-0-375-87074-3 (trade) — ISBN 978-0-375-97074-0 (lib. bdg.)
1. Apes—Juvenile literature. 2. Monkeys—Juvenile literature. 3. Primates—Juvenile literature.
I. Ruiz, Aristides, illustrator. II. Mathieu, Joseph, ill. III. Title.
QL737.P9R23 2014 599.88—dc23 2013014209

Printed in the United States of America   10 9 8 7 6 5 4 3 2 1   First Edition

Can You See a Chimpanzee?

by Tish Rabe

illustrated by Aristides Ruiz and Joe Mathieu

The Cat in the Hat's Learning Library®

Random House 🏠 New York

I'm the Cat in the Hat,
and we must not be late.
Today I will take you
to meet a primate.

Let us leave right away,
and I'll take you to see
a loris, a lemur,
and a chimpanzee.

My Chimp-mobile
will find them, I know.
re off to meet primates.
mp in and let's go!

Primates are mammals

that vary in size.

They have hands

that can grasp

and

forward-facing eyes.

Here's a fact

about primates

that really is neat—

some can hang by their hands,

their tails,

or their feet.

The three main groups of primates
I'll list here for you.
They are monkeys and apes
and prosimians too.

M = MONKEYS

A = APES

P = PROSIMIANS

proh-SIM-ee-unz

To remember the three groups
is really a snap!
Just think M-A-P—
the three letters in *map*!

First let's meet some monkeys!

Monkeys are acrobats.
They can leap in the air.
Most live in the trees.
It's safer up there.

For protection, they often
live in a group.
A group of monkeys is
known as a troop.

SNUB-NOSED
MONKEYS

10

e's the world's smallest monkey.

l me, have you met?

holding my finger—

ygmy marmoset.

e mandrill is the largest.

s a colorful sight,

th a red and blue face

d a belly that's white.

Apes have broad chests
and arms that are strong.
Apes use their strong arms
as they move along.

THIS IS CALLED
KNUCKLE WALKING.

The gorilla's the largest.
This ape walks around
on all fours, with its knuckles
and feet on the ground.

A bonobo is smaller.
Its mouth is light red.
It also has long,
parted hair on its head.

Gibbons have strong arms,
and these apes can leap
from one tree to another—
up to fifty feet!

Orangutan mothers
raise their babies alone.
Adult males spend their time
in the trees on their own.

ORANGUTAN means
"old man of the forest."

They find fruit that is ripe.
Then they sit quietly,
peeling the skin off the
fruit carefully.

Durians are fruit
an orangutan likes.
They are smelly and round
and they're covered in spikes!

MONKEY

APE

Most monkeys have tails,
but apes? They do not.
This difference between them
is easy to spot.

Now we'll meet some prosimians.
Here, look at these!
Most prosimians spend
their lives up in the trees.

Small lemurs climb trees
and like leaping around.
Big lemurs spend much of
their time on the ground.

MONGOOSE LEMURS

Arboreal
(ar-BOR-ee-ul):
living in
or traveling
in trees

RING-TAILED
LEMURS

THING
2

MADAME BERTHE'S MOUSE LEMUR

Madagascar is where all lemurs come from. The smallest is close to the size of my thumb.

ye-ayes are lemurs
hat hunt bugs at night.
hey have bright orange eyes
nd black fur tipped with white.

They have very sharp claws, and you can see that their ears stick out like the ears of a bat!

Primates don't all look alike.
This orangutan shows
its arms are so long,
they almost touch its toes.

A chimpanzee's body
is covered with hair,
but its face and its ears
and its palms are all bare.

galago has pointy ears,
round head, and round eyes.
galago and a chipmunk
re about the same size.

Proboscis monkeys have
droopy noses—like him.
This kind of monkey
can jump in and swim!

proh-BOSS-kuss

The names of some primates
can give you a clue
about how they look
and the things that they do.

Ring-tailed lemurs have tails
with black and white rings.

Hear this singing gibbon?
When he wakes up, he sings

nale silverback gorilla's

r is silver-gray.

lets baby gorillas

np on him and play.

Galagos are called bush babies,
and this is why:
the noise they make sounds
like a human baby's cry.

Tarsiers, like this one,
have long, slender tails.
Look closely. You'll see
its tail's covered with scales.

Some monkeys can hang by
their tails and not slip.
They have *prehensile* tails
with a very strong grip.

SPIDER MONKEY

22

Marmosets have long tails—
just look at his.
It's even longer
than his body is!

COMMON
MARMOSET

Apes often can swing
from tree to tree with ease,
but sometimes it's too far
to swing between trees.

So . . .   they start shifting their weight.
          They start to-ing and fro-ing.

This bends one tree near the next
so that they can keep going!

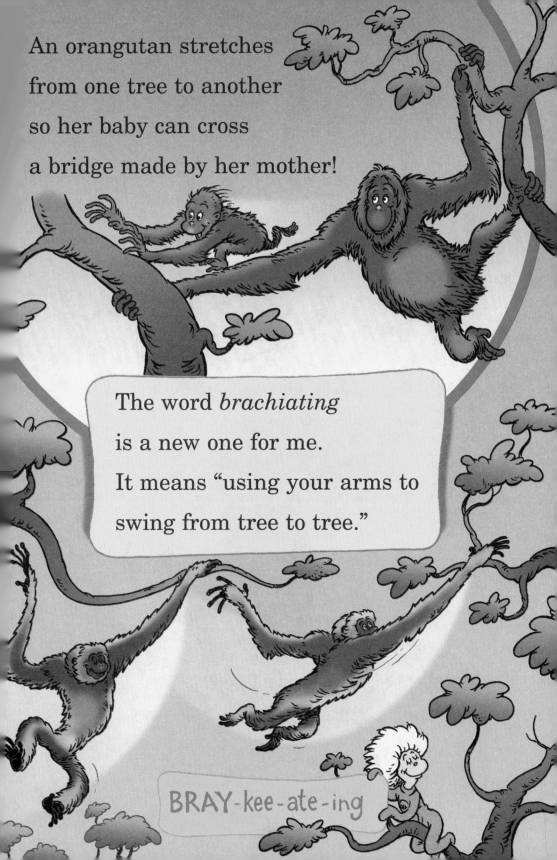

An orangutan stretches
from one tree to another
so her baby can cross
a bridge made by her mother!

The word *brachiating*
is a new one for me.
It means "using your arms to
swing from tree to tree."

BRAY-kee-ate-ing

Some primates use too
like these chimpanzees
They're using sticks
to get honey from bees.

A bonobo takes a stick and pokes it around to pull tasty termites out of their mound.

A monkey takes a rock to give a nut a smack. She does it with care so the nutmeat won't crack.

CAPUCHIN MONKEY

Monkeys depend on their eyesight.
They look carefully
to see where to land
when they jump from a tree.

SPIDE
MONK

This chimp can see colors.
Which fruit will she get?
The yellow bananas are ripe.
The green ones? Not yet.

Tarsiers can't move their eyes,
but when one hears a sound,
it can turn its head almost
all the way around!

Chimps do things people do.
They laugh, smile, and frown.
When excited, these apes
might jump up and down.

They make different sounds,
which other chimps hear—
they tell where to find food
or if danger is near.

Chimps hoot at each other
when they want attention.
Hugs, kisses, and back pats
are signs of affection.

Primates can be noisy!
Day and night, they are shrieking,
whistling and whooping,
grunting and squeaking.

GORILLA

wler monkeys start howling
the start of the day.
eir howls are so loud,
ey are heard miles away!

When a male siamang sings
a sac of loose skin
expands under his chin.
Soon a female joins in!

SEE-uh-mang

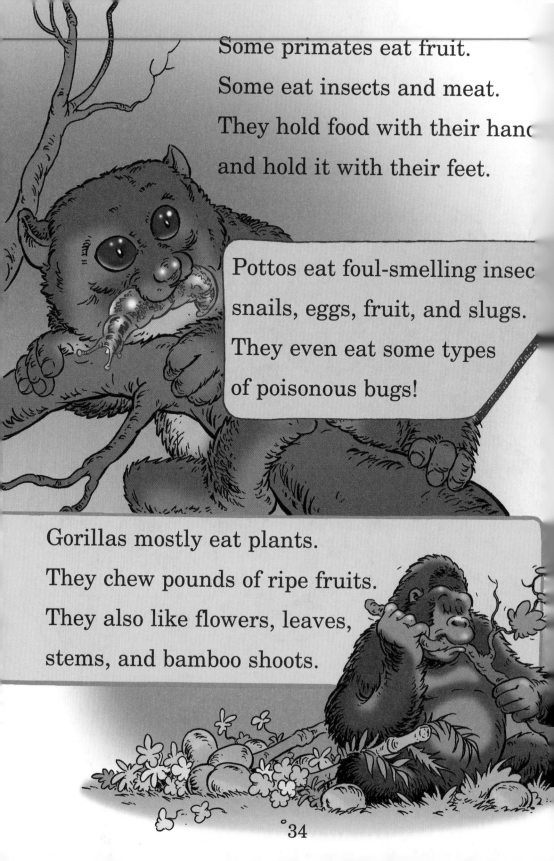

Some primates eat fruit.
Some eat insects and meat.
They hold food with their hand
and hold it with their feet.

Pottos eat foul-smelling insec
snails, eggs, fruit, and slugs.
They even eat some types
of poisonous bugs!

Gorillas mostly eat plants.
They chew pounds of ripe fruits.
They also like flowers, leaves,
stems, and bamboo shoots.

Marmosets eat insects,
sticky sap, and tree gum.
I don't think you'd like it,
but they think it's "yum"!

Tarsiers are carnivores.
They wait for their prey.
Sooner or later,
prey does come their way.

Baby orangutans have
little hair when they're b
They cling to their mothe
That's how they stay war

A chimpanzee mom
grooms her baby with care
and picks dirt, seeds, and
insects out of his hair.

Sometimes a tarsier
takes her baby and keeps
it in her mouth while
she climbs trees and leaps.

Tamarin babies
hold tight to their dad.
It's the bumpiest ride
that two twins ever had!

EMPEROR TAMARIN

When it's time for
some gorillas to rest,
they take branches and leaves
and each makes its own nest.

Gibbons don't build nests.
Instead, you can see,
they sleep sitting up
in the fork of a tree.

Zzzzz z z z

When lorises sleep,
here's what they do—
they roll up on branches
or in clumps of bamboo.

To avoid predators,
baboons sleep in high places—
way up in trees or
on narrow cliff faces.

We have met lots of primates.

Now I see two more.

They're standing right here.

Have you seen them before?

Here's a fact about primates

that's amazing but true—

people are primates!

So you're primates too!

PRIMATES

GLOSSARY

Arboreal: Living in or traveling in trees.

Bamboo: A woody, hollow-stemmed, tree-like grass in the tropics or subtropics.

Brachiating: Moving from place to place by swinging from one arm to the other.

Groom: To make something tidy.

Knuckles: The rounded joints where you bend your fingers.

Madagascar: An island off the coast of Africa where lemurs live.

Mammals: Warm-blooded animals that give birth to live young.

Nutmeat: The kernel, or inside part, of a nut, which can usually be eaten.

Prehensile: Adapted for grasping things.

Proboscis: A long, flexible nose.

Pygmy: Something that is very small.

Sac: A small bag-like structure.

Vary: To take different forms, such as the many types of primates.

FOR FURTHER READING

Face to Face with Gorillas by Michael "Nick" Nichols and Elizabeth Carney (National Geographic Children's Books, *Face to Face with Animals*). Get close to gorillas and learn why their habitats need to be saved. For ages 6–9.

Gorilla, Monkey & Ape by Ian Redmond (DK Publishing, *Eyewitness Books*). A detailed guide to the lives of the great apes, monkeys, and other primates. For ages 8 and up.

Gorillas: Gentle Giants of the Forest by Joyce Milton, illustrated by Bryn Barnard (Random House Books for Young Readers, *Step into Reading*). A nonfiction reader packed with amazing gorilla facts. For ages 5–8.

The Watcher: Jane Goodall's Life with the Chimps by Jeanette Winter (Schwartz & Wade). Follow Jane Goodall on her worldwide crusade to save chimpanzees. For ages 4–8.

INDEX

apes, 9, 12–13, 15, 24, 30
arms, 12, 13, 18, 25
aye-ayes, 17

babies, 14, 21, 25, 36–37
baboons, 39
bonobos, 13, 27
brachiating, 25
bush babies, 21

capuchin monkeys, 27
chimpanzees, 6, 18, 26,
    29, 30–31, 36
common marmosets, 23

diet, 14–15, 17, 34–35
durians, 15

ears, 17, 18, 19
emperor tamarins, 37
eyes, 8, 17, 19, 28–29

feet, 8, 12, 34
fruit, 14, 15, 29, 34

galagos, 19, 21
gibbons, 13, 20, 38
gorillas, 12, 21, 32, 34, 38

hair, 13, 17, 18, 21, 36
hands, 8, 18, 34
howler monkeys, 33
humans, 40

insects, 17, 34, 35, 36

knuckle walking, 12

lemurs, 6, 16–17, 20
lorises, 6, 39

Madagascar, 17
Madame Berthe's mouse
    lemurs, 17
mandrills, 11
marmosets, 11, 23, 35
mongoose lemurs, 16
monkeys, 9, 10–11, 15, 1
    22, 27, 28, 33
mouths, 13, 37

nests, 38–39
noises, 20, 21, 30–33
noses, 19

orangutans, 14–15, 18,
    25, 36

os, 34
nates, 6, 7, 8, 9, 18, 20,
   26, 32, 34, 40
ooscis monkeys, 19
simians, 9, 16
my marmosets, 11

g-tailed lemurs, 16, 20

mangs, 33
rerback gorillas, 21
ging gibbons, 20
ep, 38–39
ib-nosed monkeys, 10
der monkeys, 22, 28

ls, 8, 15, 20, 22–23
narins, 37
rsiers, 22, 29, 35, 37
ols, 26–27
es, 10, 13, 14, 16,
   24–25, 28, 35, 37,
   38, 39

The Cat in the Hat's Learning Library®

Can You See a Chimpanzee?

Clam-I-Am!

Fine Feathered Friends

A Great Day for Pup

Hark! A Shark!

Hurray for Today!

I Can Name 50 Trees Today!

Ice Is Nice!

If I Ran the Dog Show

If I Ran the Horse Show

If I Ran the Rain Forest

Inside Your Outside!

Is a Camel a Mammal?

Miles and Miles of Reptiles

My, Oh My—a Butterfly!

Oh Say Can You Say DI-NO-SAUR?

Oh Say Can You Say
What's the Weather Today?

Oh Say Can You Seed?

Oh, the Pets You Can Get!

Oh, the Things You Can Do
That Are Good for You!

On Beyond Bugs!

One Cent, Two Cents,
Old Cent, New Cent

Safari, So Good!

There's a Map on My Lap!

There's No Place Like Space!

A Whale of a Tale!

What Cat Is That?

Why Oh Why Are Deserts Dry?

Wish for a Fish

Would You Rather Be a Pollywog?

Coming in 2014:

Once Upon a Mastodon